Apples to Orchards

How to live an Abundant Life on an Average Salary

By Stan Dunster, M. Ed

No part of this publication may be reproduced, stored in a retrieval system, or transmitted, in any form, or by any means, electronic, mechanical, photocopying, recording, or otherwise, without the prior consent of the publisher.

Any content, information, and any materials provided in this book is on an as is basis. The author makes no warranty, expressed or implied, as to its accuracy, completeness or timeliness. Neither are any promises of results to be obtained by the recipients, implied. The author shall not, in any way, be liable to any recipient for any inaccuracies, errors or omissions herein.

Copyright 2014 Stan Dunster

Publisher: Restorev Publishing

ISBN: 978-0-9918760-0-6

Cover: Thank you Tina for your creativity.
Design by, khymeradesign.com

What others are saying

As an entrepreneur, I see many beneficial and direct applications gleaned from Stan Dunster's personal experience in this book. Practical tools for increasing personal effectiveness and for ultimately reaching your goals.

Jeff Neustaedter
Jeff Neustaedter & Associates Real Estate, Calgary, AB

What a privilege and pleasure to read Stan Dunster's book; it's a terrific piece of work, beautifully organized and shot through with an enveloping humanity.

Henry Ewert
Teacher, Author, Lecturer, Historian.

CONTENTS

Forward i
Introduction 1
Step 1 In Writing 33
Step 3 Intense Desire 45
Step 4 Benefits 53
Step 5 Starting Point 59
Step 6 Deadlines 67
Step 7 Identifying the Obstacles 83
Step 8 Knowledge Required 93
Step 9 Identify Helpful People 97
Step 10 Visualization And Self-Talk 103
Step 11 Back With Determination 115
Step 12 The Plan 123
Bibliography 133
Who is Stan Dunster? 137

Forward

That Stan Dunster has written a book entitled "Apples to Orchards; How to Live an Abundant Life on an Average Salary" is entirely as it should be, since his life exemplifies everything this book teaches. Stan and his family have set many life goals through the years, most of which have come to fruition. Before Stan and Deanna married, they resolved to achieve two major life goals: to have a family and to travel. Four children and much travel later—and fifty-five+ years of marriage—they also are able to relish five grandchildren.

Dunster's life has possessed an enviable inevitability about it because of his dedication to planning, taking life by the scruff of the neck rather than allowing life's vagaries to dictate his future. He achieved his B. Ed. At the University of British Columbia in 1959, his M. Ed at Western Washington University in 1966, then taught with surpassing energy and preparation in secondary schools for more than thirty-six years, serving as department chairman for many of those years. In addition, Dunster taught summer school in what became the British Columbia Institute of Technology as well as working in that same capacity at Simon Fraser University.

Resolving to search out travel opportunity within his chosen vocation, Dunster scored a brilliant coup when he applied, and was chosen, to teach for the Department of National Defence in Germany for two years.

On his return to Canada, Dunster continued his influence for excellence in education, serving on three curriculum revision committees, and writing two correspondence courses as well as a teaching manual for British Columbia's Department of Education. For two years, he would be the president of the B.C. Business Educators' Association, ultimately being granted, with good reason, the Sheila Cameron Award for "an exemplary and outstanding contribution to business education in British Columbia."

His dedication to adult education was emphasized by his role, for several years, as night school supervisor for Coquitlam Continuing Education, and still Dunster somehow found time to be a featured speaker at teachers' conventions in BC., Manitoba, and Arizona.

Dunster's impact in church affairs has been significant; he has functioned both as Sunday School teacher and superintendent, as well as church moderator. In military affairs he has served as platoon commander at summer camps for the Canadian Army Cadets for two summers, and has achieved the extraordinary rank of Captain in the Canadian Army Militia.

And travel? The Dunsters have certainly aced that life goal! He and his wife have relished their role as tour hosts for several tour companies, travelling throughout Canada, the United States, Europe, Japan—climbing Mt. Fuji mostly "in the dark, and the Canary Islands. Perhaps most importantly to them, they have driven every kilometre of our Trans-Canada Highway from Victoria, B.C. to St. John's, Newfoundland.

Only Stan Dunster could have written "Apples to Orchards; How to Live an Abundant Life on an Average Salary": he and his wife have indeed lived successfully by inviting the Twelve Steps of his book to become part of the very fabric of their lives, making these Steps the basis of achieving life goals. May the readers of this book be exhilarated by the service Dunster has performed by making his once-in-a-lifetime plan for success available to everyone.

Henry Ewert, 2014

Introduction

Setting goals is one of the most important things you can do to guarantee your personal, professional and financial success. Goals are like a road map to your target destination. Each goal accomplished is another mile behind you on the way to where you want to be. **Mark Victor Hansen**

A dream is your creative vision for your life in the future. It is what you would like life to become. A goal is what, specifically, you intend to make happen. Goals should be just out of your present reach, but not out of sight. **Denis Waitley**

Welcome to your REVOLUTION!

Many of you reading this book have set New Year's resolutions at one time or another. Some of you did this for fun because many of your friends were doing it, or it was just the thing to do at the time. Some of you, however, did it because you were truly serious at the time about making some significant changes in your life.

Unfortunately, fewer than five per cent of people setting New Year's resolutions successfully follow through with them. Two of the most common reasons for this are the following:

1. those who set them for fun soon forget about them; and
2. those who were serious about the changes they wanted to make did not know they needed to follow a plan.

The sad fact is many of us spend more time planning a two-week vacation than planning the rest of our lives.

If you were thinking of building a new home you wouldn't think of building it without obtaining a set of plans. Prior to getting the plans you might speak with people who had already had their own home built. You would visit homes on the market in your price range and desired location to see what kinds of things you would like to include in your new home. To get an idea of how your new home could look, you would peruse or study magazines specializing in home design and decorating. You might even create a scrapbook of the information you found.

Furthermore, you would not decide to go on a motor trip to somewhere you had never been before without at least getting a map, a list of accommodations, and even making some advanced reservations. You would want to make sure that you arrive where you want to be and are well rested and fed.

If you are going to visit some foreign lands you would do even more study on what you need to do to get there and what you want to see when you finally arrive. You would read books, visit a travel agent, watch DVDs and talk to people who have already taken a trip to where you want to go or somewhere similar.

If people spend this much time on activities that will involve them for only a few weeks or months, why don't they spend more quality time creating a map or plan for the rest of their lives? The answer, I believe, is that they are just not aware that there is a plan available for designing the rest of their lives.

Again, welcome to a book that can assist you in creating a REVOLUTION in your life.

Prior to embarking on this life-changing adventure there is something I would like you to do:

Stand in front of a full-length mirror and look yourself straight in the eye and say,... "I am going to stop complaining about my life. I am going to stop spending time with complainers. I am going to get on with creating the life of my dreams"

Say it several times and say it with genuine conviction!

You may be experiencing what many have called "the good life" and yet deep down you have the feeling that **you are entitled to so much more.** The truth is **you are entitled to more,** and it is not necessary for others to receive less so that you can have the "more" of whatever it is that you think you are entitled to.

We all have dreams. Some are more dramatic than others but up to this point you just haven't found a route that will lead you to achieving those wants or dreams.

You may want to create more financial wealth for yourself and your family. You may want to create a healthier lifestyle. You may want to travel, not just across the country, but around the world. You may want to help people that are in need. Whatever it is **you** desire, the means of attaining that desire are within you, and this book will show you how to get them.

If you follow the steps that I show you in this book with determination, you will be able to create a life for yourself that will exceed your wildest expectations.

This book has been designed to provide you with a road map. But a road map is only useful if you continually refer to it; otherwise, you could continue to find yourself lost in the wilderness.

Thousands of people around the world set and achieve their goals every day. There is NO reason why YOU can't join them on this exciting journey.

GOALS OF THIS BOOK

1. To emphasize the importance of goals and the BENEFITS TO YOU of accomplishing them.

2. To explain how goals REQUIRE EFFORT ON YOUR PART, both in their creation and in their accomplishment.

3. To provide the steps that can HELP YOU become an effective goal-setter.

The first step is for you to find out a little more about yourself.

Let's get down to business. Look at "GETTING WHAT YOU WANT FROM LIFE" below. Before you even start to read you will notice all the "YOUs" and "YOURs" that appear throughout the page. The purpose of these is to make it clear that this material is all about YOU. It is **not** about your family members, your relatives, your friends, me or anyone else. This material is all about YOU and YOUR LIFE.

I would like you now to replace all the YOUs and YOURs with Is and MYs. This may seem to be a rather silly exercise, but your mind will accept this change very readily and enable your mind to focus on YOU and what YOU want.

GETTING WHAT YOU WANT FROM LIFE

1. Choose the direction YOU want for YOUR life.

   YOU need to choose what YOU want to do with YOUR life and then YOU need to get to work to make it happen.

2. Identify YOUR area(s) of excellence.

   Identify at least one or two things that YOU do well and/or enjoy.

3. Accept challenges.

   Sometimes struggling with things YOU thought would be difficult helps YOU discover some of YOUR strengths.

4. Recognize opportunities.

   YOUR opportunities often come disguised as obstacles, problems, or hard work.

5. Strive for a balanced life.

   Set goals in a number of areas of YOUR life—don't become a limited individual.

6. Concentrate on achieving YOUR number one goal.

   Choose the goal YOU most want to accomplish in each of the areas of YOUR life and get to work on it.

Now that you have changed the YOUs and YOURs to I's and MYs, have I been able to convince you that this information is truly all about YOU?

For several years I had been reading of the successes other people were experiencing as a result of setting goals for their lives. Although these people were experiencing more success than I was, for some reason I did not do anything specific about it.

One evening, two years before our 25th anniversary, while visiting with a couple that married during the same summer as my wife and I, we came up with the idea of celebrating our 25th anniversaries together by going on a European tour.

Our family lived in Germany for two years while I taught for the Department of National Defence at one of the dependents' schools. We loved the experience and had talked many times of returning. Was this going to be the opportunity? We discussed the idea for several days and then told our friends that it was a "go" for us.

Since we would already be in Europe, we thought we might as well stay for the whole summer. Our son, who had not yet been to Europe, could then join us after we had completed the 21-day tour with our friends. Once we made the decision, we sat down to calculate the costs. The rough calculation of costs for the three of us for two months of travel came to a much larger figure than we expected. In fact it would take up a large part of a year's salary.

At this point our car was paid for, our house was almost paid for, but we had very little in the bank.

How were we to come up with the necessary funds in less than two years?

Come with me along the journey of goal setting, and I'll show you exactly how we did it (and how you can, too!).

Opening the door to the rest of your life

I have taught many seminars on goal setting. With all the wonderful opportunities that this world has to offer each and every one of us, it amazes me, how few things the members of the audience can think of that they would like to do, to have, or to experience more of. Perhaps most people have given up on their dreams because it seems to be such a waste of time to dream of that better life. **You have to learn to dream again or for the first time!**

You can face the future with anticipation or apprehension. Apprehensive people have not spent time designing their future. You either buy into your own future or someone else's. If you are serious about accomplishing anything in life, you first have to be able to clearly verbalize what you wish to accomplish. A fuzzy future has very little pulling power.

I once read about a man, John Goddard, who at age fifteen made a wish list of the things he wanted to accomplish before he died. There were approximately 130 items on his list. By the age of 47 he had accomplished 163 of these wishes. If he had not taken the time to write them down, how many would he have missed and how could he have kept score on his progress?

Every peak performer is an obsessive goal setter, motivated by compelling and internal goals.

What if there are no restrictions?

I would like you to do yourself a favour now by listing, on MY DREAM LIST provided below, some of the things that you would like to be, have, do, see, or experience **if time, money, or talent, were not a problem. There are no restrictions!**

Here are a few ideas to help you get started:

- One goal I really want is to have...
- A place I would like to visit is...
- If I had a great deal of money I would...
- I would like to be the kind of person who...
- I wish I had a better job in the _____ industry.
- My life would be better if...
- I wish I could go back to school and get a (degree, diploma) in_____
- I wish I could quit smoking (drinking, taking drugs)
- If I could start over I would...
- I wish I could drive a new...

So let's take the first step

You can always add to your list on a separate sheet of paper. I suggest you write in pencil as writing in ink gives it a sense of permanence. Pencil helps you think that you can change your mind whenever you wish. **Remember,** if time, money, or talent were not a concern to you, what would you like to be, do, have, see, share, or experience? Let your imagination run wild! Have fun! Isn't it about time?

You need to write down some **BIG** dreams that are really going to make you stretch over a number of years, some smaller dreams that can be completed in just a few years, and some still smaller ones yet that you will be able to accomplish in just a few weeks or months.

Try to write without stopping. Use abbreviations, anything to aid you in getting your ideas down on paper as quickly as you can. Your wants need to be created in a number of areas of life. This will help you live a balanced life. Here are some areas for you to consider: career, family, finances, health, intellectual, personal and spiritual. (This list is in alphabetical order and not necessarily in their order of importance).

MY DREAM LIST

1. _____
2. _____
3. _____
4. _____
5. _____
6. _____
7. _____
8. _____
9. _____
10. _____
11. _____
12. _____
13. _____
14. _____
15. _____
16. _____
17. _____
18. _____
19. _____
20. _____
21. _____
22. _____
23. _____
24. _____
25. _____
26. _____
27. _____
28. _____
29. _____
30. _____

31. _____
32. _____
33. _____
34. _____
35. _____
36. _____
37. _____
38. _____
39. _____
40. _____
41. _____
42. _____
43. _____
44. _____
45. _____
46. _____
47. _____
48. _____
49. _____
50. _____

Don't be discouraged if you cannot fill in all the lines at this time. You can come back to My Dream List time and time again.

Whenever you think to yourself, "I'd like to ..." return to these pages and write down your thoughts. There should be many of these occasions. Once again, remember that your **dreams are actually your goals in their formative stages.**

What are you afraid of?

Are you saying to yourself, "I would sure have to be lucky to have any of these dreams come true. The only kind of luck I have is BAD LUCK." Take a moment to look at, and think about, the following definition of LUCK.

Labouring Under Correct Knowledge

Once you know what it is you want to do and start preparing and doing it, you will be amazed at the amount of GOOD LUCK that will come your way.

Many of us have not experienced more success in life because of FEAR. This fear can either be fear of success **or** fear of failure. One plants as powerful a negative image in our life as the other.

False Education Appearing Real

If you plan your life you will soon discover that most of your fears are either imaginary, have already occurred, are easy to solve once they have been defined, or are beyond your control.

Are you still dreaming? Good for you!

Goals, NOT Dreams

Unlike dreams, goals are **specific, action-oriented targets** that can be **defined, discussed, visualized, and committed to writing.**

Setting goals is a lot like life. It's a journey, not a destination. It's a marathon, not a sprint.

The major reason for setting goals is to **compel** yourself to become the **person** it takes to achieve them. Possibly, one of your dreams is to become wealthy—even a millionaire. We'd all like that, wouldn't we? There are so many things you can accomplish for yourself and others if you have the necessary money. What do you think then is the greatest value in becoming a millionaire? Is it the million dollars? I don't think so. No, the greatest value is in the skills, knowledge, discipline, and leadership qualities you will develop during the process of becoming a millionaire. More money does not automatically bring security or increased happiness. On the contrary, more money can bring stress and insecurity if a person hasn't prepared for this increased wealth.

It is the personal growth you experience that brings psychological peace of mind and real wealth into your life. You will find that income rarely exceeds personal development. Your ability will grow to match your goals.

There have been many examples of the foolishness of people who have won large amounts in a lottery.

In fact, I have read in several places that approximately 85% of the people who win the million dollar- type of lottery are dead broke within five years.

This is a very sobering thought.

Having goals helps you assume more responsibility for your own life, and puts you on the right track to getting what you want from life. While you are on this journey, you will need to spend major time on major items and minor time on minor items and **learn to tell the difference.** Never get the times reversed. The farmer must pay close attention to the seasons of the year. Plant in the spring—harvest in the fall. So, too, will you need to learn to use the seasons of life:

- when to pour it on, when to back off

- when to take advantage, when to let things ride

Change is inevitable! It is neither good nor bad. It's what we make it. Developing goals helps us to control the direction of that change.

In the following chapters you will learn how to make many of the dreams on your list become a reality through the setting of your own goals for the rest of your life. As you go through the process, you will find that your goals are not cast in stone. Goals are ever evolving, ever changing.

You won't get everything you want either. It's just not that kind of world. Sometimes it will hail on our crops and rain on our parade. However, if you work the system, you'll get more than plenty, and that should be more than enough.

Here are four questions to ponder while you are working your way through this book.

> **Why?** Should I try? Should I work that hard? Share that much? Go that far?
> **Why not?** What else am I going to do?
> **Why not ME?** Who else will do it for me?
> **Why not NOW?** Get at it <u>tomorrow</u> at the latest.

Next, on the forms "MY TIME LINES", I would like you to write out your current dreams, from the "MY DREAM LIST", under three headings, Short-range, Medium-range and Long-range. Don't get too concerned with the actual length of time each heading has attached to it. Those numbers are only provided as a rough guide.

What IS important is for you to think of the types of dreams that you really want to set. Make some of your dreams large and exciting. Don't concern yourself with whether you can actually see yourself accomplishing these dreams or not in the time allotted; just write them down. Also, try to do some under such headings as Career Expansion, Family Development, Financial Freedom, Intellectual Growth, Personal Relationships, Spiritual Awareness. (*These are in alphabetical order and not necessarily in the order of importance to you..*)

At this time you should probably not share what you have written with anyone else, except perhaps a spouse or a **very** close friend who you know will support you. Later on, as you begin to create some successes you can share what is happening. At this early stage you don't need negative comments.

MY TIME LINES

In the appropriate spaces below, break down the dreams you listed on My Dream List into the appropriate time you feel you can accomplish them.

Long-range goals (more than 5 years)

1. _____
2. _____
3. _____
4. _____
5. _____

6. _____
7. _____
8. _____
9. _____
10. _____

Medium-range goals (1 – 5 years)

1. _____
2. _____
3. _____
4. _____
5. _____
6. _____
7. _____
8. _____
9. _____
10. _____

Short-range goals (1 year or less)

1. _____
2. _____
3. _____
4. _____
5. _____
6. _____
7. _____
8. _____
9. _____
10. _____

Now, please look at "LET'S GET OUR PRIORITIES STRAIGHT". On these forms you need to take the dreams from "My Time Lines" and prioritize them; that is, under each heading write the dreams in the order you would like to accomplish them.

LET'S GET OUR PRIORITIES STRAIGHT

Please note that the order of headings on this page is the opposite of those on the "My Time Lines" page because, as you have probably already discovered, often short-range goals lead to medium-range goals which lead to long-range goals.

Short-range goals (less that 1 year)

1. _____
2. _____
3. _____
4. _____
5. _____
6. _____
7. _____
8. _____
9. _____
10. _____

Medium-range goals (1 – 5 years)

1. _____
2. _____
3. _____
4. _____
5. _____
6. _____
7. _____
8. _____
9. _____
10. _____

Long-range goals (more than 5 years)

1. _____
2. _____
3. _____
4. _____
5. _____
6. _____
7. _____
8. _____
9. _____
10. _____

The next exercise, "MY IDEAL WORKING DAY" may pose a problem for some of you as you may still be in school or college. Some of you may have been working for only a short time. Others may have been working for a number of years.

No matter, you are going to get a job, and probably all of us can envision a job where we will hardly be able to wait to get to work every day. Correct? That is the job you need to write about here.

You are not writing a paragraph for your English teacher so relax. Dream and write down your ideas in point form. You don't need to worry about spelling or punctuation or whether your verbs agree. Good English is important; it is just not important at this point. Your thoughts don't even need to be in any special order. Try to use as many of the five senses (see, hear, smell, taste, and feel) as you can in your description.

Don't be afraid to take all the time you need to do this. You are not in a race. The more ideas and the more precise your ideas are, the better they will assist you. You may even want to use additional paper.

MY IDEAL WORKING DAY

_____
_____
_____
_____
_____
_____
_____
_____

APPLES TO ORCHARDS

STAN DUNSTER

APPLES TO ORCHARDS

Didn't that feel great! Wouldn't it be wonderful if that was what is would be like when you arrived on your job tomorrow? It isn't likely going to happen by tomorrow, but it is something you can be working toward as we progress.

Now go to "MY IDEAL NON-WORKING DAY". This should be a really fun exercise. We have all dreamed about this type of day when we don't have to go to WORK. Now is your chance to put these ideas on paper. You may have several ways you would like to spend your non-working days. **GREAT!** Put them all down. The same instructions that you followed for the previous exercise apply here also, especially the one about using your five senses. Just have fun!.

MY IDEAL NON-WORKING DAY

_____
_____
_____
_____
_____
_____
_____
_____
_____
_____
_____
_____
_____
_____
_____
_____
_____
_____
_____
_____
_____

STAN DUNSTER

APPLES TO ORCHARDS

STAN DUNSTER

APPLES TO ORCHARDS

I hope YOU have done a lot of thinking and had a huge amount of fun while you have been completing the last few exercises. Some of you may be saying, "This is just a waste of my time. These things will never happen for me." Not true. There is hardly anything you cannot achieve if you have a well-thought-out plan to get it. **Goals such as you have been writing about are coming true for thousands of people every day.**

Although this book has 12 steps, the steps do not need to be completed in numerical order. All you need to do is to just jot down any ideas that fall under a given heading when you think of them and then you'll have them written down for when you can fit them into your plan.

Step 1

In Writing

The first step to success begins with me, a piece of paper and a pencil or my computer.
Brian Tracy

The finest thought runs the risk of being irrevocably forgotten if we don't write it down.
Arthur Schopenhauser

Goals are critical to success, and learning how to set them is of utmost importance. There is one point on which all experts on goal setting agree: **it's vital that you write your goals down.**

If you don't put your goals in writing they are still only wishes and dreams. Wishes and dreams are goals in their formative state. Not writing them down simply avoids making a commitment.

All truly successful men or women that I ever met or read about have one thing in common. At some point in their lives, they sat down and wrote out their goals. The first great key to success begins with you, a piece of paper and a pencil. **Keith DeGreen**

Concrete and tangible

Writing out your goals helps you to organize your thoughts, to identify clearly exactly what you want. They become concrete and tangible. You can pick up a piece of paper, look at it and touch it. As you write out the different steps in setting your goals, you will find that your excitement intensifies, and your faith and belief deepen in the recognition that the goal is really achievable.

When you put your goals in writing, write them exactly as you would like to see them in reality—clearly, vividly, and in as much detail as you can. Write them in the present tense, as if they have already been achieved. Make the description of the outcome as perfectly as you can. The more specific you make your goal, the more direction they will provide. It is important that you **decide exactly what it is that you desire, and not worry about how you are going to achieve it.**

Decide what it is that you want before you decide whether it is possible or not.

While you are writing out your goals, you will have the opportunity to check to see if there is any conflict among them. For example, there is likely going to be some conflict if one of your goals is to increase your net worth several times and another goal is to play golf four or five times a week. The golf games will come, but not as you start out to greatly increase your net worth.

At this point, on the GOAL SETTING form, I would like you to write out a one- or two-line statement of your goal, such as...

I no longer smoke, and I also no longer experience any kind of nicotine cravings.

I now weigh 120 pounds and look and feel fabulous.

I now have a financial plan in place that will allow me to achieve my goals.

I am now registered in the program I need to achieve my promotion at work.

Post short-term goals where you can see them regularly

Once you have selected the goals you want to begin working on and you've written them down, transfer them to 3x5 cards. Carry these cards with you. Read them over and over during the day.

Put a copy of the goals on the side of the mirror in front of which you shave or put on your makeup each day. In this way you'll be able to look yourself in the eye as you are repeating your goals at the beginning of each day. Every time you repeat a goal, the stronger it becomes in your subconscious. You could even have a set of cards on your bedside table so you can refer to them just before you go to sleep and/or as soon as you wake up. If you are constantly aware of what your major goals are, you won't lose sight of them as you proceed with your whirlwind of daily activities.

Keep daily to-do lists

Our memory fails us too often if we don't write things down. So, each evening, before you go to bed, write a list of things you need to do the next day, your "To Do List", so to speak. Many of these items need to be steps to take in achieving your goals. You need to work on at least one small step toward reaching a goal every day. Not only does this help you organize your day, it gives you great satisfaction when you can cross off your accomplishments during the day.

> *If you're not working on your goals, you are working on someone else's.* **Jim Rohn**

Now you have started on the plan for YOUR future.

At the end of each chapter you will add to these forms, and at the end of our time together you will have completed the outlines for several of your goals. If you don't have a computer, you can photocopy several sets to use.

At the end of each chapter I'm going to share exactly how we used these same steps to achieve our goal of a European Tour for our 25th anniversary, so you can see how these ideas work.

What did the Dunsters do?

Since at the time I didn't understand what I was really supposed to do. I created a large "thermometer" and attached it to the refrigerator door. Up both sides I pasted pictures representing the various items for which we had to raise money for the cost of the tour, airfares, hotels, meals, entrance fees, and so on. This was our way of writing out our goal.

NOTES:

Step 2

Believable

Be not afraid of life. Believe that life is worth living and your belief will help create the fact.
William James

Ah, that a man's reach should exceed his grasp, or what's a heaven for?
Robert Browning

Most of us go through life accepting what life gives us if it doesn't require us to reach too high or bend over too far. We just don't believe enough in ourselves to make that little extra effort. Many of us have been told not to try too hard because we'll just be disappointed in the end.

I must accept myself as I am right now, but recognize that I have the ability to be someone better.

Most people don't give themselves the credit due for things they have already accomplished.

Whenever you see yourself climbing the ladder of accomplishment, understand that where you are

now is OK, but you are capable of climbing so much higher.

Don't pick a starting target that is eighty percent better than you've been doing up until now, as this high target will only discourage you when you are beginning.

In the beginning, you need to challenge yourself to do just a little better than you are doing at this point in time. A 10 percent improvement may be the maximum you can start with. Soon you will discover that you will be able to reach higher in several areas of your life. So our next step is to decide if the goal we want to work on is truly believable for us. In most instances it will be even if you don't believe that right now.

There are some exceptions. For example, if you are "five foot two with eyes of blue" you are never going to be a centre for an NBA team, no matter how much you desire to be one.

There are other basketball positions you can get if you love the game. When I was teaching, one of the shortest male teachers on my staff was the basketball coach and a very successful one at that. He could coach, but he couldn't play centre. If basketball is the love of your life there are many basketball related occupations that can connect you with the game.

At the other end, if you are six foot nine, you are never going to be a jockey. No matter how much you desire to be a jockey it is NOT going to happen. There are other horse-related jobs you will be able to do, perhaps not so visibly, but related to horses all the same.

The Challenges of life

Life is like that—despite what we may say, we want to be challenged. We want life to be challenging, but not impossible. Remember, many golfers have actually made a hole-in-one, and that is what keeps the rest of us playing the game.

Unfortunately, many of us make up stories to justify why we cannot achieve our life goals.

I once read the story of a very short lady who wanted to become a surgeon. Her fellow students laughed at her goal as she was far too short to comfortably reach over the table and the patient. Not to be stopped, she asked why she could not have a platform built to stand on while she was operating. Someone built it—she stood on it—end of the story.

Accept yourself as you are right now—imperfect, changing, growing, but truly worthwhile. Recognize, too, your uniqueness; you have the ability to develop and maintain your own high standards.

Expectations

Seldom does an individual, team, or group exceed its own expectations. That's why most of us should invest in a life coach. A student once earned a B in my course and proceeded to tell me that I must have made a mistake. I checked my records and she had indeed earned a B. When I asked her why she felt I had made an error with her mark, she replied that she had never had any mark higher than a C in her life. On her next report I gave her what she deserved, a C.

If we have self-limiting beliefs, regardless of whether or not they are based on reality, to the degree to which we believe them, they become reality for us.

Most people do not aim too high and miss—they aim too low and hit. The creative subconscious seeks to maintain expectations, not surpass them. What about **your** expectations? What do you believe about **yourself**? You have the power to take control of many more aspects of life, both mental and physical, than you ever thought possible.

You must believe that you **deserve** to reach the goal and that you **will** achieve it when you are **ready** for it. You must nurture your belief until it turns into an absolute conviction that you **can** attain your goal.

Challenging, but realistic

Remember, when you are setting your goals, especially at the beginning, you must absolutely believe that you have the ability to reach these goals. There should be at least a 50/50 probability of success. Make them difficult enough to be challenging, but believable enough to be attainable, Too easy, and you will not think them worthwhile. Too difficult, and you will become discouraged

If your goal is to earn more money over the next year, set a goal that is perhaps 10, 20 or 30 percent higher than your current income. These are realistic numbers. If your goal is too far beyond anything you have achieved in the past, such as doubling your income, it becomes a demoralizer. Since the amount is so much larger, you will seem to be making little or no progress. You will then become discouraged and stop believing it is possible for you.

You must set goals high enough to pull you, but not so far beyond you that you lose heart before you even begin.

Whatever the mind of man can conceive and believe, it can achieve. **Napoleon Hill**

He was not, however, speaking of unrealistic goals. Big goals are different from unrealistic goals. Big goals are simply a series of short- and medium-range goals. Sometimes it will take months or years of preparation and hard work to achieve a big goal. However, if it is a worthwhile one, it is worth the patience and persistence necessary for its achievement.

The problem is not so much what you truly desire and can't do, but rather what you don't put down on your list of desirable goals because you feel it is impossible to achieve them. You will be surprised that what you now think is impossible can become possible if you approach it in the correct way.

What did the Dunsters do?

We realized that thousands of Canadians travel to Europe every year. If they felt it was believable for them it was believable for us.

Step 3

Intense Desire

Desire is the starting point of all achievement, not a hope, not a wish, but a keen pulsating desire which transcends everything.
Napoleon Hill

When you know what you want, and you want it bad enough, you will find a way to get it.
Jim Rohn

How badly do YOU want to achieve YOUR goal?

When we are talking about intense desire we are talking about saying to yourself, **"I want this so badly it hurts"** rather than, "It would be nice if I could get this."

Wishing for something to happen will not make it happen. YOU must really want it to happen. YOU must have an intense desire. No, I have not made an error with the way YOU is printed. I want to emphasize that the goals you set must be for

YOURSELF. Doing something because someone else wants you to do it, for most people, will not have sufficient driving force to make it happen. If it does happen it will be at a much lower level of intensity than if it is something YOU really want for YOURSELF.

There is only one success—to be able to spend your life in your own way. **Christopher Morley**

Your goals must be personal and for yourself. Other people may benefit from your achievements, especially if they affect other family members, but YOU need to be the number one beneficiary.

Be yourself, but a new self

Many of us go through life doing things that other people want, not the things we want for ourselves. We go to university or college because our friends are going or our parents want us to, even though what we really want to do requires some other form of training. We dress as someone else wants to see us dress, read the books someone else wants us to read, work at a job that someone else wants us to work at.

Sometimes this works out because the people making the suggestions are wiser and more experienced than we are. This is especially true for some young people who may lack experience in some areas of life.

Although no one else can really set your goals for you, before you discard ideas from others, be certain that you have given both their ideas and your choices some considerable thought. But in the end, you have to set your own goals. Some young people, and older people too, do the opposite to what has been suggested just to show their independence.

Don't become discouraged by what others may say about your choices. If you really want to do something—go for it. In most cases, unless your behaviour needs to change radically, you are better off if you do not share your goals with anyone else at the beginning. There are two exceptions to this however:

- people, such as your parents, coach, boss, or spouse whose help you will need to achieve your goal, and
- other goal-oriented people, the kind of people that will encourage you in the direction you want to go—your cheerleaders, if you like.

What really excites you?

Look back at MY DREAM LIST. What things jump off the page and make you excited? Remember, you are not deciding whether it will be possible, only that it gets you excited just thinking about the possibilities. Many of you have had your past dreams ridiculed. Some of these earlier dreams may have been put back into your subconscious, on the back burner, if you like. Try to pull them forward again.

There may be some, however, that you have suppressed because you could not see any way to accomplish them. Now that you are working on goal setting you might want to re-examine them. In fact, you may find yourself getting really excited about them once again. Go back to MY DREAM LIST and start writing down the ones you thought of that now truly excite you. This book will be taking you through a variety of steps that will improve your chances of success with those things you intensely desire.

Perhaps there are also some goals that you are no longer interested in. Let them go. Clean house.

You need to realize that YOU need the will to win.

Desire is the secret

The necessity of supporting a family is not a strong enough motivator to make you form the habit of doing things you don't like to do for the very simple reason that it is easier to adjust ourselves to the hardships of a less satisfactory way of life than it is to adjust ourselves to the greater hardships of creating a more satisfactory way of life.

You need the will to win. You can have everything else in the world going for you, and if you don't have the desire to be somebody, if you don't want to go out there and change your own destiny, there's no hope for you. But if you do, if you want your goal badly enough, no obstacle can stop you. The intensity of this desire provides the pressure to sustain focused thinking and single-minded purpose. This is the first step because unless you truly desire something you will be unable to muster the mental focus needed to follow through with the other steps.

Where will you allow your desires to take you?

- **Desire** gains strength when it is in the concrete form of a goal.

- **Desire** becomes an obsession when you think about it all day, every day.

- **Desire** becomes a commitment when you do at least one thing a day that propels you toward your goal.

- **Desire** becomes endurance when you see small successes growing into larger ones.

Don't let losers, criticizers, and complainers change you and make you give up.

Attitude isn't just a little thing; it's everything!

Achieving many of the goals you will set for yourself will make it necessary for you to work overtime for your ultimate benefit. This may be overtime at work or extra time you are spending in your spare time on developing other goals for yourself. This extra effort may be inconvenient in the short term, but the benefits can last forever.

Thousands of people get up early to go fishing and thousands stay up late to party. Can you make the same sacrifice for YOU?

I spoke about New Year's resolutions earlier. The problem with most people setting New Year's resolutions is that they don't get them fixed inside their heads. They don't really know why they are setting them in the first place. It's just a fun, spirit-of-the-moment thing. There is the desire of wanting to fit into the activities going on around them—one of which is making New Year's resolutions. But, where is the real DESIRE to accomplish them?

Turn to your GOAL SHEETS and under INTENSE DESIRE write down how great your desire is to complete each of the goals you have chosen.

Here is a starting idea for you:

I <u>really</u> want to achieve (you insert your goal). "I want it so badly that I can almost taste it" as the saying goes. I am prepared to do the very things that will succeed in bringing this (you insert your goal) into being in my life. I understand that it will not always be convenient or comfortable now, but I will be well rewarded in the future.

Write out the intense desire you have for each of the goals you have chosen to work on at this time. Don't use my words; try to use your own. Be sure to use personal pronouns as often as possible. You can make it much more meaningful as your **desire** is all about **you**.

We are here to start a REVOLUTION in our lives. We are not taking part in a game played on New Year's Eve. We are SERIOUS.

What did the Dunsters do?

After spending time discussing the pros and cons of taking the trip to Europe, we knew without a doubt we REALLY wanted to go. We also did not want to lose face by telling our friends that we couldn't afford to go.

The INTENSE DESIRE was there.

NOTES:

Step 4

Benefits

Life is not to be endured, but to be enjoyed.
Senator Hubert Humphrey

Always do your best, what you plant now, you will harvest later. **Og Mandino**

Now that you have chosen the goals that you want to work on at this time, decided that you have an intense desire to achieve them and that they are believable for you, the next step is to list the benefits that you will experience when you achieve these goals.

Will you be wealthier? Will you be healthier? Will you have a better job? Will you own a nicer home? Will you have developed better interpersonal skills? Will you be a better all-round person?

I am certain that if you have decided on what your goals are and have made it this far in the book, you can think about all kinds of benefits that will come your way while you are working to achieve your goals and once you have actually achieved them. You will also find that many other benefits, perhaps not even related to your goals, will come your way.

Perhaps you will meet a new person, read a great book, or see a special television program. Sometimes the benefit might be new clothes or a nice dinner or a trip. These are all benefits to you. When you are working on your goals, you will find that things and opportunities will appear that you weren't even thinking about.

What gets you going?

What truly motivates you? Recognition? The feeling of winning? Your family's well-being? Benevolence?

What you desire is a powerful motivator **only** if there is a good reason behind it. Some goals you once thought were important may lose their appeal because you can't find enough benefits to warrant the effort needed in achieving them If you can find enough benefits you can do spectacular things. It's the benefits that make the difference.

Big reasons

Some people are motivated by money, or the possibility of driving a flashy car, or living in a beautiful house. Others are motivated by recognition, or status and prestige, or by the idea of earning the admiration of others.

Are **your** reasons big enough? Is your desire intense enough? Is your belief strong enough? If you can answer yes to these questions, nothing can stop you. Reasons come first, solutions come second.

Becoming a new person

The major reason for setting goals is to **compel** you to become the person it takes to achieve them. Remember, a person who becomes a millionaire through planning and hard work has a far different attitude toward money and life than the person who becomes a millionaire through winning a lottery. That's why 85% of people who win the big lottery are broke within five years. When you are looking for benefits to reaching your goal, be certain to include some self-development benefits.

One of your tasks in this process is to keep your desire burning brightly by continually thinking of all the benefits, satisfactions, and rewards you will enjoy as a result of achieving your goals. Take pride in what it is that you are accomplishing.

List ALL the benefits

The more benefits you can list, the more worthwhile and achievable your goal will become. These benefits will also act as magnets to draw more and more ideas to help you. Now is the time for you to focus on the benefits you are looking for. You may want to look back at "IMAGINE YOUR IDEAL WORKING DAY" and/or YOUR IDEAL NON-WORKING DAY" for some inspiration to get you started. The more you can list, the more worthwhile and achievable your goals become. These benefits will also act as magnets to draw more and more ideas to help you.

Choose appropriate rewards

We all want some kind of reward for our achievements. Perhaps it will be in the form of raises or gifts, better health, no fear at opening bills, less chance of cancer ...

Think of ways you can reward yourself and those helping you in achieving your goals. But, be sure the rewards are appropriate. Small gains, small rewards. Large gains, large rewards.

On your GOAL SHEETS start a list of all the tangible and intangible benefits that you will enjoy as a result of achieving your goals. The longer the list, the more motivated and determined YOU will become. One or two reasons won't provide much motivation. Ten or twenty reasons for achieving your goal and you will become unstoppable. Of course, you can keep adding others as you think of them.

What did the Dunsters do?

We were excited about the opportunity to revisit people and places from our previous time in Europe. There would also be so many new places to visit and new people to meet. It was also going to be a great opportunity for our son to be visiting Europe for the first time.

We recognized many benefits and we were excited about the planning and the trip that was ahead. Of course, the big reward would be the trip which would enable us to visit some of the places we missed seeing the first time we were in Europe. There would be the joy of showing our favourite places from last time to our son, as well the our pride of being able to introduce him to old friends who'd not yet met him. The delight in enjoying some of our favourite foods again – wiener schnitzel in Germany, fresh warm, oven crisp baguettes in France, traditional pizzas in Italy, and so on.

NOTES:

Step 5

Starting Point

"Determine your NOW—then determine your FUTURE." **Author unknown**

The way to get started is to quit talking and begin doing. **Walt Disney**

Most of us don't give ourselves credit for the things we have already accomplished in life. We tend to focus on what we haven't done instead of focusing of what we have done in the past and are willing to do in the future.

There are two sides

One side needs you to list what you have already learned in life so far.

The other side needs you to determine when you are going to actually get started <u>working</u> on your goals.

Transferable skills

Don't minimize the importance and value of what you already know; things like who you know, and what you have already accomplished in your life. In many situations when you begin to work on a goal, you will find that you are already well on your way to achieving that goal.

If your goal is to save a certain amount of money, how much have you saved to this point? If it is a particular job that you want, what necessary skills do you already possess? If you plan to travel to a particular place, what do you already know about travelling and/or the place you want to visit? Seldom will you have made no progress toward your goal. However, if you don't determine your starting point, how can you measure your progress?

Many of us possess skills that, while not directly the ones needed for our current goal, are transferable skills. You want to be a long-distance truck driver. Do you have your basic driver's license? Can you read a map? Can you stay awake for long periods of time? These are skills you need for truck driving that you probably already have. Now you can concentrate on those that you may not possess such as dealing with air brakes, backing up a large trailer, and turning tight corners with a large rig.

If you want to be a lawyer you need to be able to persuade people, you need to be able to speak in front of a group of people, you need to have a good memory. If you don't already have these skills, they are ones you can concentrate on learning long before you get to law school.

People skills

Start developing a skills list of <u>anything</u> you do well. It's always helpful to ask people you regularly come in contact with about any skills they see you already possessing. We all have one or more areas in which we are outstanding—areas of excellence, if you like. What are your interests? What holds your attention? Do you write well, encourage people, approach people easily; are you a good listener? How are you at managing people, money, a business, or a household? Do you have organizational skills or teaching/coaching skills? Are you intuitive, nurturing or inspirational or all three? Do you feel good when you are doing things that you like or are good at? True self-esteem comes only when you have a deep-down feeling of competence.

Here is a list of miscellaneous words that you may find describe things you do well or are natural abilities you possess: organizing, listening, nurturing, inspiring, coaching, problem solving, public speaking, good team player, learning, training, decision making, logic, reasoning, intuition, writing, selling, computing or communicating.

Knowledge list

Another list you can make is one that describes knowledge you already possess: formal or informal education; specialization in something present or past; other ways of doing business, e.g. internationally or on the Internet; knowledge of literature or music; cultural understanding; or an understanding of human nature. What are your interests? What holds your attention? What do you find inspirational? Do you know how to write well? Can you manage a team of people? Is your life organized?

In other words, what knowledge do you already possess that can benefit you as you develop a team of people to help you set new goals for your life?

Relationship list

Yet another list you can develop is one of relationships: direct family members; current and past friends; people in your business including customers, vendors, advisers, outside contractors; people you worked with or for in the past; people who have been beneficial to you; people you do, or have done business with or for in your personal life; college friends; and neighbours. At this point you may not want to list people you are nervous about approaching. Write them down anyway. As you proceed, you will become bolder and then you will feel more comfortable in approaching them.

Creative skills list

A final list, for now anyway, is one that deals with skills that call upon your more creative side. Do you have mechanical ability? Are you good at repairing things? Can you create things in wood, ceramics, clay, glass, or stone? Can you sew? Do you have the ability to paint with water colours or oils?

As you complete these lists, you will begin to see yourself with more dimension and ability. You will see new possibilities emerge. You will become empowered. You will recognize abilities you possess but have never opened up to. Now you will begin to look at life and yourself with a broader, deeper perspective.

Time to get started

Go to your GOAL FORMS and in the Starting Point section start filling in the skills you already possess. Don't be shy about what you are putting down. Don't rush this. As always, you can come back and add and change anything you want to. Don't minimize the importance and value of what you know, who you know, and what you have already accomplished.

Here are some thought-starters to help you get started on listing knowledge and skills you already have. I've listed some very basic things you may not have thought of:

If you are in your senior years of high school you are farther ahead in your education and know so much more than those young children that are in their primary years.

Have you already opened up a savings account and put some money away? There are many people around you that haven't done that.

Have you ever played on a team or coached one? Just think of the teamwork skills you have developed.

Were you ever on the executive of a club? You have developed some leadership skills and people-managing skills.

Have you ever taught classes for a religious or community group? You have developed some teaching skills. Right?

As a homemaker you have you have learned how to manage people and things, organize a task or even a day, do basic bookkeeping. These provide you with basic skills on which to build.

Most of us don't give ourselves enough credit for the things we have already accomplished in life. We tend to focus on what we haven't done instead of focusing on what we have done and are willing to do in the future.

Now is the time to make your lists Don't hesitate to list your accomplishments, big or small, to date. Don't be shy. Give yourself the credit due. I did this once and came up with more than a loose leaf page of things. Some were small, some were big, but they were all about ME. This activity surprised even me. Get writing and surprise yourself.

Here is a quote I have posted above my desk:

> *"I don't have to get it right, I just need to get it going.* **Mike Litman**

As you work on this, keep asking yourself these questions: Where am I coming from? Where am I going? Where do I want to end up?

NOTES:

Step 6

Deadlines

We didn't lose, we just ran out of time.
Vince Lombardi

Goals are dreams with deadlines.
Diana Scharf Hunt

Deadlines go a long way toward helping to motivate you to work harder to reach your goals. It is much easier to reach a goal if you are able to measure and generally know how close you are to achieving your goal. The feeling of moving toward your goal helps to make you feel like a winner.

If you haven't set a deadline for accomplishing your goal, it is not a goal at all; it is still only a dream. Take the time to calculate a reasonable time within which you should be able to accomplish the goal.

Are deadlines really important?

Suppose you were to walk into a furniture store and explain to the salesperson that you want a particular bedroom suite. She then explains the various payment options available.

You counter with, "I want an open-ended contract. Of course I intend to pay for the suite, but I want to feel free to pay what I can when I feel I can afford it."

The salesperson looks at you and says, "WHAT!"

I think you can see where I am going with this. There has to be a deadline for both parties.

Setting those deadlines

There is no point to what you have written up to this point if you have not actually set a date for the accomplishment of your goal.

If it is a monetary goal, there are financial tables available to help. If it is an educational goal, it is fairly easy to find out how long it should take, attending full- or part-time. Ask someone who has already obtained the desired education or speak to a school counsellor. With a little diligence, you should be able to set an appropriate deadline for each of your goals.

Once you have set the deadline for the accomplishment of a goal, work backwards from that date to the present and begin to set some short-term goals and deadlines.

If, for example, you want to lose a certain amount of weight over the next six months, set some weight levels that you'll need to achieve in, say, two-week increments. I need to warn you that really tight intermediate steps might be somewhat discouraging if they are not reached precisely, especially in the beginning. However, if your goal is to lose twenty pounds and half-way through your time-line you have lost only eight pounds, that may be just fine. On the other hand, if you've lost only two pounds, some additional changes in your eating and exercising habits are going to be needed.

Uncomfortable but not impossible

Don't set a date months ahead if you know in your heart of hearts that you can easily reach the goals much sooner. The sooner, the better. If you are not stretched working on your goal, you are not going to become the better person you need to become to benefit from the goal you have set.

Deadlines only on tangible goals

Set deadlines on all tangible, measurable goals, such as increases in income or net worth, or losing a certain number of pounds, or running a certain number of miles. When you set a deadline for tangible goals, you program them into your subconscious mind, activating your subconscious forcing system, which ensures that you accomplish your goal by that date at the latest.

On the other hand, don't set deadlines on intangible goals, such as the development of patience, kindness, compassion, self-discipline, or other personal qualities. When you set a deadline for the development of personal qualities, this same forcing system ensures that your deadline will be the first day you begin to actually demonstrate the quality you've chosen.

When deadlines are set for us, we have to meet someone else's deadline. For example, in school, whether you are in public school or post secondary school, the term comes to an end at a specific date, whether you are ready for it or not., If you are planning a trip that is to leave on a certain date, that is the date on which you have to leave, even though you may not have everything in place.

Clay, not concrete

What if you do set a goal and a deadline and then you don't achieve it by the deadline you've set? Simple. You set another deadline. It just means you're not ready yet. You guessed wrong. You were too enthusiastic or optimistic. What if you don't achieve it by you new deadline? Simple. You set still another deadline until you finally achieve your goal. As the sales trainer says, "There are no unrealistic goals, only unrealistic deadlines."

The fear of not achieving a goal by a deadline is often a major concern. It is probably one of the biggest reasons why people don't even set goals. If you have been doing your best in the achievement of your goals and the time has run out, change your deadline a bit. If, on the other hand, you have been goofing off, give yourself a shake. Take another look at the goal you have set to see if it is <u>really</u> what you want. Think seriously about the whole thing through the steps you have written down. Make any necessary adjustments and re-set the deadline.

Just be careful that if you extend a deadline you do so for a good reason, not just because you didn't follow through with your original plan. You have to be quite tough on yourself when setting goals. The good thing is that when you have been setting them for some time, it becomes easier and easier, almost automatic. Why? You have become a better person.

> *There are no unrealistic goals, only unrealistic deadlines.* **Don Huston**

With a goal that has a two-, three-, five- or ?- year deadline, you need to break it down into six-month goals, then take these and break them down into monthly, to weekly, to daily goals. That is, you start with the visualization of the goal as already accomplished and work back, in gradually shorter intervals, to the present, all the time setting appropriate deadlines. Then ...

Do at least one thing every day toward the accomplishment of each of your goals.

"I believe that time runs out for most people because they keep saying, 'My time's gonna come,' and all of a sudden, it's over and they didn't pick out one thing to go for. Life is just a flicker, and it's flying by. It's not waiting for some special time when it's going to stop and be our time." **Source unknown**

This deadline step can be a tough one, but I know you are up to it. When you set the deadline for your goal, make it stretch you. Remember the saying, "Out of reach, but not out of sight."

Remember, you can change what you have written any time you wish. It's not the fact that you didn't reach your deadline, but rather the reasons you didn't reach it that are important.

The world isn't going to stop and wait for you.

What did the Dunsters do?

The deadline was set for us. July 1 was the date our flight was going to leave for Europe. The plane was leaving whether we were ready or not. We sat down and worked backwards to fit in the various steps we were going to need to take: tickets, hotel reservations, traveller's cheques and so on, and wrote down some dates.

Get out your calendar and your GOAL SHEETS and set some deadlines for the goals on which you are working.

DO IT NOW!!

Take a break at this point and give yourself a chance to go back over what you have written in all the steps up to this point. Carefully read over any notes you have made and make any changes you feel necessary at this time. Perhaps you feel more confident now than when you started and you want to upgrade the thinking you had earlier. Can you think of more dreams to write on your DREAM LIST?

_____
_____
_____
_____
_____
_____
_____
_____
_____
_____
_____
_____
_____
_____
_____
_____
_____
_____
_____
_____

Where We Are Now?

You have now reached the half-way point in your goal-setting quest. Before we move on, let's take a few minutes to recap what we have accomplished so far. You will then have the opportunity to take the final steps in your goal-planning guides.

Goals are set in three time periods

Long-range goals: those requiring five or more years to achieve.
Medium-range goals: those requiring one to five years to achieve.
Short-range goals: those requiring less than one year to achieve.

Try to set goals covering all lengths of time. I realize that your long-range goals require you to set medium- and short-range goals. That's not what I'm talking about here.

Be sure to set some goals that can be <u>completed</u> in less than one year, for example, to graduate from high school, to decorate a room or to go to Hawaii. Goals like these, which can be accomplished in a relatively short period of time, are confidence builders. They will encourage you to stretch yourself to set and work toward long-range goals in the near future.

Goals are set in a variety of areas

Goals should also be set in a variety of areas of your life, for example, personal, family, social, financial, spiritual, physical, business, academic, and emotional.

Each of us has at least one quality that makes a difference. We all have the capacity to be excellent in at least one area of our lives. But, to become the person you really want to become and are capable of becoming, you need to become a well-rounded individual. That means you need to work on goals in several areas of your life at the same time. From time to time you will stress some goals over others. However, always remember to have a variety of goals moving along at basically the same time. It makes life more interesting, too. It is much more interesting to watch someone juggle a ball, a plate, and a hat than someone who is just juggling three balls.

When you are starting out, you may want to try only three balls. As you gain experience you will want to try adding other goals to make life interesting.

If taken seriously, completing these activities is going to change you. You will need to be willing to change your mind set. Then you will decide to look at life with a broader and deeper perspective.

**Have enough <u>reasons</u>.
Reasons come first; answers, second.
<u>You</u> define, <u>you</u> describe, <u>you</u> work, <u>they</u> pull.**

You have been working on goal-planning guides. Using the summary below, along with what you have already written, try to make what you have said as clear as you possibly can. Hopefully you are working on at least three goals in at least two time periods.

A Review of the Steps in Setting Goals

Do not share your goals with anyone who is not involved in helping you achieve them.

In Writing – Check to see that you have written out your goals clearly and vividly and in the present tense **as already achieved.** Have you written them on 3×5 cards? A picture on the refrigerator door? Notes on your mirror? A dream book? (See Chapter 10)

Intense Desire – Explain to yourself, in as much detail as you can, **why** you want to accomplish these goals.

Believable – Here is where you get the opportunity of telling yourself why **you <u>can</u>** accomplish these goals.

Benefits – You need to be really creative here. Think long and hard of **all the benefits** the accomplishments of these goals will bring. If you can only think of one or two benefits, perhaps you need to re-think your goal. If you have many benefits to write down, get out of the way—achievement is coming.

Starting Point – You are probably already part way to accomplishing your goal. You've already completed writing down the above steps. Haven't you? You've **already** accomplished a great deal in your life. Write down those accomplishments as they relate to these goals you are working on.

Deadline – **When do you plan to accomplish these goals?** You need to do some serious thinking here. Don't be too hard or too soft on yourself. **Just be realistic!**

Do it and let **it** speak for you.

If you have not done so at this point, complete the sections we have been investigating. Make enough copies now and complete one for each of the goals you have chosen to work on.

My Goal Setting Plan

Copy the forms and complete them with the information you have at this time.

Since some of you may still be having difficulty setting more than one or two goals for yourself. That's O.K. This is new to about 95% of the population; it takes time to get a good grip on what is going on. I've listed some more suggested goals that may be helpful to you. Use them as is, or change them in any way that will be helpful to you. Better still, create your very own.

Career Goals

- Become president of the company by age forty.
- Get promoted this year.
- Find another career more in line with my tastes and aptitudes.
- Open my own restaurant.
- Get transferred to home office.
- Become the top salesperson in my district.
- Get my boss' job.
- Get a job with my company's competitor.
- Complete the CGA program.
- Quit work and become a college professor.

Personal Relationship Goals

- Devote two hours each day to getting to know my children better.
- Take at least one escape weekend every three months with my spouse.
- Try to meet at least one new person each day.
- Convert a former adversary to a friend.
- Fall in love.
- Get married.
- Cultivate one new, close friendship each month.
- Learn to remember names.

Recreational Goals

- Go on a safari.
- Register on the Internet.
- Buy a boat/motor home/tent.
- Write a novel.
- Take a trip around the world.
- Raise dogs/cats/birds.
- Watch the sunset in _____

Personal Growth Goals

- Learn one new word a day.
- Take a speed-reading course.
- Learn to make better use of my time and energy.

- Attend a lecture a month on something I know little or nothing about.
- Take up conversational French.
- Go away to college.
- Volunteer for charity work.

Material Goals
- Be financially independent in five years.
- Buy a house this year.
- Get a sports car.
- Buy an excellent stereo system.
- Buy a motorcycle.
- Buy a yacht and live on it.
- Acquire rental property.
- Add another bathroom to the house.
- Earn enough money to pay off the mortgage.

Social Goals
- Join the golf club.
- Make the dean's list.
- Graduate with honours.
- Run for political office.
- Wear expensive clothes.
- Move to an impressive neighbourhood.
- Throw formal dinner parties for important people.

- Be captain of the football team.
- Be chosen employee of the month.
- Appear on radio or television as an expert.

You know by now that these aren't really goals. They are really only dreams or goals in their formative stage. Now your job is to take whatever you want from this list and any other lists you may have and turn them into **goals for YOU.**

We have now arrived at the second set of exercises that are to take us to the successes we are so anxious to achieve.

Step 7

Identifying the Obstacles

One of the greatest surprises you'll experience is when you discover that you can do what you were afraid you couldn't do. Your obstacles will melt away, if instead of cowering before them, you make up your mind to walk boldly through them.
Max Steingart

One of the secrets of life is to make stepping stones out of stumbling blocks. **Jack Penn**

What are some of the obstacles with which I am likely to be faced?

Death and taxes

There are always obstacles! What are obstacles? What are **YOUR** obstacles? Obstacles are those obstacles you see when you take your eyes off your goals.

We've probably all heard these jokes about opportunity. "Opportunity often comes dressed in work clothes", or "opportunity appears as hard work." Are the work clothes an obstacle to you? Does hard work turn you off? Does the grass look greener somewhere else? The grass is **NOT** greener somewhere else. If you doubt this, read the book *Acres of Diamonds* by Russell H. Conwell.

Even when you are walking down the street you can come upon obstacles. There may be a toy lying in your way. There may be a piece of pavement missing. If you are keeping your eyes open you can easily deal with such obstacles. If not, you could hurt yourself.

When you are focused on what it is that you want to accomplish, you often will find that what you originally saw as an insurmountable wall will turn out to be nothing more than a bump in the road.

As you develop your goals it's a good idea to develop a list of the possible obstacles you expect to face. Put this list in order of significance. Then prioritize the steps you need to take to overcome them.

Determine the number one obstacle that may be keeping you from accomplishing your goal and focus on overcoming it. Create goals that will help you do this. Then, do the same for each of the other obstacles that appear. When written down, obstacles that once loomed large can now look much smaller. Recognize, too, that obstacles can, in fact, be just the challenges necessary to your success.

If, as you work on your goal, you experience no obstacles between you and your goal, it is probably not a goal at all, but merely an activity.

Internal or external

The obstacles may be internal or external, within the situation or within you.

If they are internal you need to be honest with yourself and ask, "Is there something about myself I will have to change? Is there an ability or skill I will have to develop?"

If they are external, the wrong job, the wrong company, the wrong relationship, you may need to start over.

Sometimes you may feel good about your job, but you find that you are not getting ahead as quickly as you would like. You need to identify what it is that is holding you back and then do everything possible to eliminate it. Let's say you are in sales and your goal is a higher income. You will be limited by the size and number of your sales. The limiting factor to increased sales could be the number of calls you make or the number of new prospects that you generate. On the other hand, it might be your inability to ask for an order.

Doing things you don't like to do

Since many fail, or settle for less, what achievers do must be unnatural. If it was natural, we'd all have no trouble doing it. The secret of success for **every** person who has ever been successful lies in their forming the habit of doing those things which failures don't do.

There are some things in life that seem to be absolute givens. This is one of them: when you are experiencing success, don't get in the face of your friends and co-workers. Just change your attitudes slowly so that those around you can gradually adjust to the new you.

Change negatives to positives

Here is a list of some negative traits (obstacles), some of which you may possess. Look over the list and pick out two or three that you feel you possess and in the space provided at the end of this section, quickly write out some goals for eliminating them or turning them into positive traits.

I lack initiative.
I don't express myself well.
I can't handle responsibility.
I'm not assertive.
I'm not strong (mentally, emotionally, or physically).
I can't think clearly.
I have to work twice as hard as most people.
I rebel against authority.
I'm lazy.
I'm disorganized and undisciplined.
I'll go crazy if I don't keep busy.
I can't work without supervision.
I'm not a good worker.
I'm unworthy of an important position or promotion.
I'm sarcastic and abrasive.
I have insufficient education.
I have insufficient capital.
I have too many dependents.
I am not physically attractive.
I have a bad credit rating.
I suffer from drug/alcohol abuse.
I chose an obsolete occupation.
etc., **etc., ETC.**

If you have admitted to the obstacles you may face and created some short- or medium-range goals to overcome them, you may even find that if you stay in focus, some of the obstacles may not even show up.

Rain and Hail

Bad things do happen to good people.

Cities and towns around the world plan for, and put on, their annual parade knowing full well that in some years it is going to rain on their parade.

Farmers keep on planting their crops, knowing that hail or drought has destroyed their crops in the past and will do so in the future.

We can't spend a lot of time worrying about what **might** happen.

It IS going RAIN on your parade. It WILL HAIL on your crops.

One thing that is going to happen for certain once you begin to set goals is that many obstacles are going to rear their ugly heads. Knowing that this is going to happen, makes you better prepared to deal with them.

Some of these obstacles are going to be clear to you right now, and others will appear as you progress through the exercises and when you take those scary action steps that are so vital to your success.

Now is the time to begin a list of the obstacles you think you might encounter and get prepared to deal with them.

Every obstacle is a stepping stone to success.
Author unknown

One major obstacle that you need to be aware of is that many people don't want you to be more successful than they are. There are some things in life that seem to be an absolute given. This is one of them

Putting the change process to work

Add the obstacles you think are going to be a challenge to you as you proceed on each of your MY GOALS pages.

View all problems as situations needing improvement, temporary inconveniences, or opportunities to grow.

If you play golf, you know that the ultimate aim is to make a hole-in-one. What are the chances? They're not very good, are they? Yet every day, regardless of the weather, thousands of men and women play with that ultimate goal tucked away in the back of their minds. In a recent Christmas card one of our friends related that her husband had made two holes-in-one in the past year, giving him a total of three for his lifetime. Three holes-in-one in I don't know how many rounds of golf. Three holes-in-one and he doesn't plan to stop trying.

What are the obstacles in the way of achieving this goal? First, the ball is very small, as is the head of the club. This causes some people to miss the ball completely or hit it at an angle that sends it in an undesirable direction. Next, the holes are hundreds of yards apart. In fact, they are so far away they are difficult to see and they are marked with a flag. When you do reach the green, you discover that the hole is little bigger than the ball.

Not only that, but between you and any given hole may be sand traps, water hazards, trees, and tall grass which all seem to reach out and grab at you ball. Despite all this, people continue to go day after day to chase that elusive goal—the hole-in-one.

I am working on a new game that is based very closely on the game of golf. These are the changes I am planning in order to make it easier to get that hole-in-one.

1. Make both the ball and the club head larger.
2. Move the greens much closer together so that they are clearly visible.
3. Eliminate all hazards—straight down the middle every time.
4. When you get the ball on the green, you will find that the hole is much larger than the ball. It will be almost impossible to miss.

It seems to me that with these changes, it will be possible to make several holes-in-one in every 18-hole game. Don't you think that people will flock to play my new game? Certainly not! Why not? You are right; there is not the challenge that there is in the real game of golf.

NOTES:

Step 8

Knowledge Required

If a little knowledge is dangerous, where is the man who has so much as to be out of danger?
Thomas Henry Huxley

The beginning of knowledge is the discovery of something we do not understand.
Frank Herbert

What background will I require?

Academic requirements

You don't have your high-school graduation? Find out how you can get it through the GED program.

You will probably need to obtain a copy of an academic calendar, which lists the requirements for obtaining a degree or diploma. Contact the appropriate institution.

Make an appointment to meet with a counsellor at the institution of your choice. Be sure you have all the questions you can think of **written down** ahead of time. Some of the questions you should ask, besides the ones directly related to your courses, might be the following:

- are any of these courses transferable from other institutions?
- are any of these courses offered in the evening, on weekends, or on the Internet?
- is there financial aid available, and would I qualify?
- is there tutorial help available? (this may be especially helpful if you have been away from school for a while)
- do I qualify for life experience consideration?

If you are working and can't see yourself taking time off to take more training, look into evening or on-line classes.

The Internet

The Internet can be a HUGE help to you. Not up to speed on using the Internet? There are dozens of books in the libraries or bookstores that can help you in learning about this. Often libraries offer free or inexpensive classes.

Libraries

You need TWO libraries in your life!

Personal Library

If you are going to improve your life you need to read a lot. Each time you pass shelves of books in a store, check it to see if there is a book that you should read to improve yourself. Visit used book stores to get books at a better price. Check out Amazon.com or Coles.com to see what they may have on sale.

When you are reading your own books, highlight parts that are important to you. This way you can quickly skim through the books later to refresh your mind.

All readers are not leaders, but all leaders are readers. **Harry Truman**

Public Library

A library card to your local library is one of the most valuable things you can possess. It doesn't cost much, probably less than the cost of one book.

Not only does the public library have books, but it will have CDs and DVDs on many topics you will find helpful in this quest. Of course, the CDs can be played in your car as you drive, saving you lots of time.

Many public libraries also offer programs that may be helpful to you.

NOTES:

Step 9

Identify Helpful People

You've got to ask. Asking is, in my opinion, the world's most powerful and neglected secret to success and happiness. **Percy Ross**

Success is asking for help when I need it and acting on my own when I don't. **From a wall of a recreation centre in Berkeley, California.**

Which people can I approach for assistance?

Making a list

Start making a list of <u>anyone</u> you may think can be of help to you. Add names to the list as they come to you. Probably you won't need the help of everyone on your list but it is better to have the name and not need it than to need it and not have it.

If your goal is to begin a satisfying career, former teachers and counsellors are good sources of information if you haven't been out of school too long. Human resources counsellors in your work place can help you get ahead by explaining the steps that you will need to take if you want to get promoted. If you want a promotion, be prepared for the new position <u>before</u> the position becomes vacant. Don't expect your boss to wait until you get yourself qualified.

If you want a better car, speak to a variety of car salespeople to find out prices, methods of payment and options you may be interested in. Get some brochures to study. This information will be invaluable to you when you begin to visualize your goal as already accomplished later on.

Most of our goals are not unique to ourselves. Many others have had the same goals. Our goals may have some personal qualities that apply just to our situation, but basically, these goals have been done before. Who have achieved what you wish to achieve? How can you find out how they did it? Did they write a book? Has someone else written about their accomplishments that you can refer to? Have they made an audio or DVD that you could listen to? Could you get a personal interview?

Remember to thank

You should never expect people to help you unless you can compensate them in some way. Often this compensation can simply be in the form of genuine praise for something that you have heard that they have accomplished. Sometimes it will cost you money such as when you ask for financial advice from a trained financial adviser. Sometimes just a thank-you letter or card will be enough. Before attempting to gain their cooperation, ask yourself, "What am I going to do to thank them for helping me?"

The thank-you note

Let me tell you of two employment situations with which I was personally involved.

One evening I received a telephone call from a person I knew well. I knew he had recently had an interview for a job and that he had been short listed. He was upset as we talked because the short list had been reduced to two people and the other person got the job. What was the deciding factor? The other person sent a thank-you note for the opportunity of having an interview.

Had I ever heard of sending a thank-you note after an interview? Yes I had. In fact I told all of my students to do this. How many did it? I don't know. One did it for certain. Read on.

The second situation involved one of my students. As usual I had told her to have an appropriate thank-you card ready to mail immediately after an interview. The day of her interview was a Thursday, and she was told that the decision would be made on the following Wednesday. The interview was over and the card mailed. On Monday she received a telephone call asking when she could start work. She was puzzled as she thought they still had several people to interview. When she asked about this, she was told that no one had ever sent them a thank-you card after an interview, so they thought she must be special and they wanted her to come and work with them.

People want to help

Successful people are usually flattered that someone thinks enough of their accomplishments that they will ask their advice. Be sure that you have the questions you wish to ask written down so that you will not waste the other person's time and so that you will ask all the questions you need to at the time of the interview.

Biographies

Find some biographies at your local library on your specific area of interest and related fields and <u>read</u> them. There is no need for us to learn everything from scratch. We can find out the problems and successes others have experienced and save ourselves a lot of time, effort, and frustration.

School/human resources counsellors

One of the jobs of these counsellors is to help you when you are experiencing difficulty in the spot where you find yourself at present. Another is to help you to either improve yourself in the company you are presently working for, or to encourage you to find better opportunities somewhere else in the company or in some other company.

People who are already <u>successful</u> in your field of interest

While you are working on your goals you will be amazed at the people who will unexpectedly cross your path. Since your radar is out, you will finally hear and see things that have been there all the time but you just weren't focused on them and the help they could provide.

How are you making out with the development of the lists of Obstacles and Knowledge. Remember, you certainly do not have to have all the answers right now. You should frequently be adding to these lists in the future.

This is the time to create a list of <u>people</u> you will want to contact before you get too involved as well as while you are proceeding with your investigations. You will be amazed at the number of people that will be glad to help you once they find out what it is that you are trying to accomplish.

Now turn to IDENTIFY HELPFUL PEOPLE on your GOAL SETTING SHEET and start listing those people you think will be helpful to you.

What did the Dunsters do?

We read many books and pamphlets on the countries we were planning to visit. We also spoke with the travel agent who was making the arrangements for the tour about the things we would need to do for the second half of the tour with our son. In addition, we spoke to people who had travelled in Europe more recently than we had.

Step 10

Visualization And Self-Talk

Get the picture of what you want and keep telling yourself that you're going to get it.
Claude M. Bristol

Imagination is everything. It is the preview of life's coming attractions. **Albert Einstein**

We are getting close to the end of the goal setting/achieving process. Hang in there with me.

A big obstacle you will face is visualizing yourself in a new role—the role of the successful person. You've got to look at yourself as someone with possibilities and opportunities. You've got to see yourself as a winner.

At the beginning of this program I asked you to look at yourself in a full-length mirror. Do you remember who you saw in that mirror? Look in that mirror now. Hopefully the person you now see is someone who looks confident and poised, in control of their destiny, forward looking, and on track.

Visualization is an activity that will really get your goal-setting on the fast track. We've already discussed writing out your goals as vividly as possible and as though they have already been achieved. To add even more power to you goals, you need to create a clear <u>mental picture</u> of your goal as it would appear as if **already achieved.**

Every day, visualize yourself **winning** even if you haven't yet decided on the path you want to go. Sit down for a few minutes each day and close your eyes. **See yourself the way you want to be.** Visualize yourself owning your own business or changing your job. See yourself paying off all your bills every month and having money left over. See yourself with $50,000 in your savings account, or $100,000, or whatever your goal is. Then replay these pictures over and over on the screen of your mind. Each time you do this you increase your desire and intensify your belief.

What you see

Several years ago, a comedian, Flip Wilson, would dress up as Geraldine. Geraldine's favourite expression was, "What you sees is what you gets." This has a lot more truth in it than Geraldine ever imagined.

Once you set your goal, your mind instantly monitors self-talk and environmental feedback about the goal. Let's see how we can intensify this.

A **visualization** occurs when you picture, in your mind's eye, how things will physically appear while you are working on your goal, and especially when you have actually attained it. This can be helped by creating a dream book or a dream map.

Let's talk about these two things for a minute.

First, we'll start with the **dream book.** Purchase a one-inch loose-leaf binder and some blank loose-leaf paper. If you are developing your goals in your own handwriting get some lined and blank paper. The blank paper is to be used to mount any pictures you might want to add to your binder.

Let's consider a goal for purchasing a new car. Go to the local auto mall and look at a number of different makes and models of cars. Ask for some booklets on the car of your choice. Then cut out pictures of the car you want to own. Put the pictures of the new car you wish to purchase on the left-hand page.

The written visualization, expressing the excitement you will experience using this new car, is written on the right-hand page. Describe things like how the inside of the car looks, smells and feels.

Actually go and sit in the car you want and take it for a test drive. Describe how it feels when you are out on the road, some of the road trips you want to take in it and so on. In this way, when you open to the pages describing your car you can see the pictures on the left and feel the excitement when you read the words on the right.

My wife and I have followed the same format for other goals we have set, such as the goals for our charitable giving and travelling. It works well for us and we have heard and read about many other goal setters who have used a similar approach.

As you turn the pages of your dream book, picture yourself on each page. Think how you will feel. Smell the smells, taste the tastes, hear the sounds, and then see the results on your mind's movie or television screen.

The **dream map** is developed in a similar way and for the same purpose.

Get a large piece of paper or Bristol board that you can obtain in an office supply store. Find and cut out pictures similar to what you did for your dream book.

Put a picture of yourself and/or your family in the centre of the paper. Some people cut out headlines from newspapers and magazines and add them to the mix. They are words such as *wow, great, inspiration, fantastic,* and so on.

On the map, you can paste the pictures in a random manner or you can choose sections of the paper on which to put pictures of your new car, the vacations you are going to take, or the school or college you are planning to attend. Because it is your map, design it in any way that will create desire and momentum for you.

Put it on a wall where you can see it every day. This map is similar to our thermometer on the refrigerator door I wrote about earlier. This proved to be very successful for us and we didn't even know what we were doing at the time.

Get some mileage out of your dreams. Focus them, in living colour, on the end result. For example, imagine how it will feel when you earn that degree. Visualize the graduation ceremony, feel the handshake, and hear the applause. Be specific, cover all the details. Try to attend a graduation ceremony at the institution of your choice and picture yourself as one of the graduates walking across the platform.

Do you realize that everything in the world that has been made has been pictured in someone's mind before it could be made? Just take the example of a chair, a basic chair with four legs, a seat, and a back. Such a piece of furniture could not be created unless someone first visualized what it was supposed to look like when finished.

Vivid visualization

Usually I don't ask people to share their goals with me, as sometimes they are very personal and I do not want to invade anyone's privacy. However, one year I asked the students in one of my classes to write out a goal that they could share with the class and with me. Two girls chose to set the goal of buying a car. Let's briefly look at what they said in their goals.

The first girl simply said she wanted to save $5,000 so she could buy a Corvette.

The second girl said she wanted to save $30,000 to buy a specific make of Japanese sports car. She had gone to the local dealer and chosen the car she wanted. She stated the colour of the exterior and interior and she had brought home brochures of "her" car. She sat in a similar car, rolled down the driver's window, put her arm on the window ledge and pretended how it would feel to be driving it down the street. She even had the salesperson take a picture of her in the car. She described the wonderful smell of the new leather, she checked on the horsepower, and she looked in the trunk.

Now, which girl do you think will be most likely to reach her goal? I would put my money on the second girl even though the car she wanted was apparently six times as expensive as the first girl's car. The first girl had not even found out the real cost of a Corvette.

Some helpful ideas

The steps you have already completed in your planning up to this point have given you the details of an absolutely clear picture that you can repeatedly replay into your subconscious. Your visual images become your reality and an increase in any one of the following elements will accelerate the rate at which you create the physical equivalent (reality) of your mental picture.

Frequency – How often you visualize a particular future even has a powerful impact on your thinking, feeling, and acting.

Vividness – Your early thoughts will likely be vague and fuzzy. As you think more about your goal, your mental pictures will become clearer and clearer.

Intensity – Increasing the amount of emotion with which you accompany your visualizations is like stepping on the accelerator of your potential.

Duration – The longer you can imagine a desired future event, the more likely it will happen.

Since your subconscious mind cannot tell the difference between a real experience and one that you vividly imagine, keep up the visualization and self-talk.

More tips

Affirmations

- Keep them positive, in the present tense, and personal.
- All change is from the inside out. All change begins in the self-concept. You must become the person you want to be on the inside before you see the appearance of this person on the outside.
- Tell the truth in advance. e.g. I **am** a non-smoker.

Verbalizations

- Verbalize aloud, with other cooperating people, or alone in front of a mirror.
- Speak clearly and emotionally.
- Anything you say aloud with conviction and enthusiasm has much more impact than if you speak it quietly to yourself.
- Record your visualizations onto your iPod and play them over and over, especially first thing in the morning and last thing at night.

Acting the part

- Behave as if you have already achieved the goals you've set for yourself.
- When you feel positive and optimistic, your feelings will generate actions and behaviours consistent with them.
- "Fake it until you make it."

Feeding Your Mind

- Read books and magazines for personal and professional development.
- Listen to educational CDs and watch educational DVDs.
- As you improve your inner understanding, you improve your outer results.

Associating with Positive People

- Get around the right (supportive) people.
- Fly with the eagles instead of scratching with the chickens.

Teaching Others

- You become what you teach.
- You teach what you are.

Put at least one positive statement for each of your goals on a card and carry it with you every day. As you **read** your statements, **visualize** yourself as having already achieved them. When one of the statements comes true, replace it with a new one. Do this until you have reached your goal.

Recapping

Picture myself as already in possession of the idea.

It is important that when I am setting goals that I have a feeling as to how it is going to look, feel or sound.

Get an EXACT picture in my mind of the desired outcome

The more exact my picture, the more attraction it has. I could cut out figures from magazines doing the things I want to be doing, or looking like or sounding like when I achieve my goal. I can then replace the head or face of that picture with my own.

Develop a Dream Book and/or a Dream Map with pictures and comments and look at them regularly.

These are both visuals that I can look at often to remind me of what it is I am working for.

Concentrate my attention on where I want to go, not away from where I want to be

All my attention needs to be on how I see myself when I have reached my goal. I will not focus on where I am starting from. My past is done and gone. My future is bright and exciting.

Once you set your goal, your mind instantly monitors self-talk and environmental feedback about the goal.

Now you need to create some visualization and self-talk statements and add them to your MY GOAL sheet.

What did the Dunster's do?

Since, at the time, we weren't aware of most of the suggestions given above, we pretty well stuck with our thermometer on the refrigerator door as our visual encouragement. As the money became available we filled up its stem. Pictures were added to the door. It may not have been pretty, but the refrigerator door was very meaningful to us.

Of course, we read some books and talked with some people. Obviously we weren't as prepared as we might have been, but we were learning.

Step 11

Back With Determination

Do it trembling if you must, but do it! **Emmet Fox**

The fact is, that to do anything in the world worth doing, we must not stand back shivering and thinking of the cold and danger, but jump in and scramble through as well as we can. **Richard Cushing**

You've spent a lot of time setting goals and planning strategies to get to this point. Now its time to put everything you've done into **action.** Not only do you have to take action now, but also you have to keep on keeping on. The best plan won't work unless you do.

This is called <u>determination</u> and it is going to be tough at the beginning.

Making the first move may be the most difficult step for some of you and for others it may the consistent effort required to continue to move your plans toward completion.

Think about trying to push a stalled car. Getting it to start moving is the most difficult part of the process. Once it has overcome inertia, the pushing becomes much easier. It is the same with getting started on your goals.

Making the first move

Getting started for some people may mean going from a dead stop to actual physical movement toward the goal.

Do the things you fear, and the death of fear is certain. **Napoleon Hill**

Progress always involves risk; you can't steal second base and keep your foot on first. **Frederick Wilson**

Most of us fear taking that first step because we're afraid of failure or rejection. There will be no second or third step if you don't take the first one. All the planned steps are useless without action on your part. Despite all your efforts, you will never get used to rejection, though it does become much easier to live with.

If you have never done much with your life or even if you have been living a very successful life, the initial movement on the goals you have been setting now may be very difficult for you. You are stepping into the unknown. You are possibly trying to overcome your biggest obstacle, **inertia**, and it is right there at the beginning of your attempts. It may be of some comfort to you to know that everyone else has experienced the same feeling.

Once you actually get moving you will have many successes. It is easy to keep at a task when you are experiencing success. The difficulty comes when you experience disappointment, especially when it occurs several times in a row. Earlier I stated you never truly get used to rejection; let me add that you never get used to disappointments either.

Taking stock

What if you fall short of your expectations? No matter how perfect the plan appears on paper, there may be setbacks. Maybe it is time to take stock. Are you maximizing your efforts? Is your plan realistic at this time? Have the conditions changed?

One of our big mistakes is sometimes mistaking movement or activity for achievement. Is what you are presently doing with regard to your goals truly heading you in the right direction? Are you expecting success every time you attempt something? There is no record of anyone achieving great success without many setbacks.

*If you aren't successful yet, it is because
you haven't failed often enough.*
A. Ward Ford, the first president of IBM

I think one of the best examples of persistence and determination in action occurs when watching a baby learning to walk. How many times does a baby fall and pick itself up and try again? It keeps on until it is successful. If we had given up on learning to walk as quickly as we give up on some of the other things we attempt, most of us would spend our adult lives crawling about on all fours.

Are you setting aside time each day to concentrate on your goals? Do you visualize and list your priorities each day? Are most of the items on your To Do List leading to the accomplishment of your goals?

You need to work from your To Do List all the time and the items on it must be prioritized. Physically cross each item off as it is completed and say to yourself, or out loud if no one is listening, **"Gotcha"**.

It takes time and excitement

How long have you been trying. It is said that it takes at least 21 days to change a habit. Have you given your efforts enough time to take hold or at least make a **good** start? Almost anyone can do anything for thirty days. Can you? Did you?

Are you growing in yourself? Are you trying to reach magnificent goals while being content to remain a mediocre person? For things to go better for you, you have to get better in yourself.

Are you excited about what you are doing? Once I walked past the room of an English class where the students were studying "Hamlet". The teacher was so excited about what he was doing that I stopped for a while just to listen. When I peeked in through the door's window, I saw students actually caught up in the studying of this exciting story. I studied "Hamlet" years ago, but there was no excitement in the teacher or the students in that class. If you lack enthusiasm then your subconscious, which is always aiding you if it receives the correct messages, will lack enthusiasm too.

Reward yourself

The things I've written about aren't easy. Where have I promised easy? Nonetheless, they are important. If you are into receiving rewards, plan a reward or celebration upon the accomplishment of each of your goals. Be sure it is an appropriate one. Remember what I said in Step 4. "Small rewards for small achievements". Large rewards for great achievements.

Several years ago I heard about a husband and wife who worked very hard to pay off the large balances on their credit cards. The day they paid off the last balance they decided to reward themselves. So ... they decided to go out to a nice restaurant for dinner. Nothing wrong with that. They also decided she needed a new dress and he needed a new sports jacket. Nothing wrong with that. The problem was they put it all back on their **plastic.** <u>Now there is certainly something wrong with that</u>. You get the idea don't you?

Reasons not to quit

If you find yourself on the brink of throwing in the towel, think about the following comments before you actually do quit. You've learned a lot just getting to where you are. Your experiences have developed you into someone with a better-than-average chance of success. Think of all the sacrifices you've made trying to go for it. If you quit now, all that you've worked so hard for will mean little.

Art Williams, who went from being a high school football coach to becoming a multimillionaire in the life insurance business and, in the process making many of those working with him millionaires wrote the following:

You've set your goals and made plans that involved your whole family. Can you live with yourself if you fold up your tent and go home?

Confession time

Many times I have read and heard that you should never give up on your goals. I must confess that I sometimes have a problem with what has been said. Is there ever a time when it makes sense to give up? Perhaps. If you're no longer excited about what you are doing, if you've given more than a reasonable period of time, if you've been focusing on success, if you've revisited your plan, and things still aren't working out for you, then perhaps you'd better set it aside <u>for the time being.</u>

Maybe you still need to grow some more and then revisit your plan. Don't beat yourself up. Get on with another of your goals. If at a later date you want to revisit the goal that got away, more power to you.

How hard am I prepared to work to accomplish this goal?

All day, every day, I must keep the details in mind.

If I don't keep focusing in my mind what it is I want, soon everything I have worked for up to this point will start to fade. That is why I must write goals on cards and carry them with me.

Every day I must do something that will move me closer to achieving my goal.

Since I have made a list of the steps I need to take, I can just work my way through the list, putting today's steps on my To Do List.

I must remember to put my goals where I can see them daily.

I put them on my mirror, on my bedside table, and on cards in my pocket or purse.

Step 12

The Plan

By failing to plan, you are actually planning to fail ... by default.

The trouble with many plans is that they are based on the way things are now. To be successful, your personal plan must focus on what you want, not on what you have. **Nido Qubein**

Hopefully, you have now completed all the steps in your goals plans. Look them over to see how you can perhaps add more information or do some rewrite work to make what you have already written so that it makes your intentions clearer and/or more exciting.

Are you using the five senses words: see, hear, smell, taste and feel?

This all about **YOU!** Make sure you have given your plans your very best effort. That way you will get the best results.

I wish you every success in the journey(s) on which you are embarking.

Remember, when you plant a seed you don't see the flower until many weeks have passed. Setting goals is not a quick fix, but rather a process of achieving things in your life which will make you a better person in whatever you strive for.

Just do it. **Nike**

AND IN CONCLUSION ...

Congratulations for making it to the end! I hope you feel it has been a worthwhile journey. You should now be equipped to make some big improvements in your life. It is now up to you.

For the last time here is a goal-setting outline for you.

Goal Setting

At the beginning, do not share your goals with anyone who is not involved in helping you to achieve them!

Goal – Write out your goals clearly and vividly and in the present tense as **already achieved.**

In Writing – This is where you describe how you want to write out your goals, on 3×5 cards, pictures on the refrigerator door, notes on your mirror, a dream book. The more ways you are able to think of to write down your goals the better. Completing the goal guides provided is a good way to start, but it is just one way.

Believable – Here is where you get the opportunity of telling yourself why you can accomplish these goals.

Intense Desire – Explain to yourself, in as much detail as you can, **why you want to achieve** these goals.

Benefits – You can be really creative here. Think long and hard of **all the benefits** the accomplishment of these goals will bring you. If you can only think of one or two benefits, perhaps you need to re-think your goal. If you have many benefits to write down, get out of the way – accomplishment is coming.

Starting Point – Probably you are already part way to accomplishing some of your goals. You've already completed writing down the above five steps, haven't you. Also you've **already accomplished** a great deal in your life. Write down your accomplishments in relation to these goals.

Deadline – When do you hope to accomplish each of your goals? You need to do some serious thinking here. Don't be too hard or too soft on yourself. **Just be realistic!**

-o-o-o-o-o-o-o-o-o-o-

Obstacles – What is holding you back from achieving your goals? **Be honest.** Don't talk yourself out of a better tomorrow by making the obstacles appear as mountains rather than as mole hills.

Knowledge Required – Start to **build a bibliography** of useful materials. Visit libraries. Visit used book stores. Cut our and file valuable articles. **Buy** books that you feel will be particularly valuable to you and begin building your own success library.

Help Required – Who do you know that has already achieved the goal that you are working to achieve for yourself? Most **successful people** will gladly spend time helping someone who is making plans to make some significant, positive changes in their life.

Knowledge Required – Start to **build a bibliography** of useful materials. Visit libraries. Visit used book stores. Cut out and file valuable articles. **Buy** books that you feel will be particularly valuable to you and begin building your own success library.

Visualizations/Affirmations – Keep adding pictures to your dream book. Look at it often and **picture yourself** right there in the picture. Visualize how you will feel when you stop a negative habit and replace it with one that is positive. Start making a collection of quotations that stress the kind of habits and attitudes you are trying to embrace. Read them **aloud** whenever you get the chance.

Determination – Earlier you wrote down that you had an intense desire to achieve some goals. You are now going to work hard on your determination to carry them through.

The Plan – You are building your plan as you complete your Goal Setting Guides. Be as specific as you can on the ways you see yourself heading in your quest. Check lists are good tools to use as you work your plan. **"Plan your work and work your plan."**

NOTES:

The Dunsters' next six steps

Our first six steps for achieving the goal of two months in Europe are found in Introduction. Here is how we handled the next six steps as we went about getting ready for Europe.

Obstacles - Since we had too little money to pay for such a grand vacation without using some of our savings, we looked for ways to overcome this obstacle. There was a second obstacle I'll tell you about later.

Help – Two new part-time positions opened up that made it possible for me to make the necessary money. This was a result of people I knew. The amount these two positions paid was almost exactly the amount we needed for the trip.

Knowledge – We read travel books, we watched travelogues on television, and we practised our basic tourist French and German.

The Plan – Our group tour was organized for us. For the part when our son was to join us, we went over maps and with the help of friends, books, and the travelogues, we mapped out our travels for the other five weeks. We even reserved and paid for all our hotels in advance.

Visualizations – The chart and pictures on our refrigerator door made us constantly aware of what we would be seeing and doing during the summer.

Determination - Each time we paid for something such as airline tickets, tours, and hotels we increased our determination to have a great summer.

How did it all turn out for us? I thought you would never ask.

Money was for us, as for many people, our biggest obstacle. I want to spend a bit of time explaining how we made out with the money situation and our other **big** obstacle.

1. We cut back on our every day spending.

2. A new position in my school district was advertised. It required me to work two evenings a week during the school term. I applied and I was successful.

3. A textbook representative for a California publishing company was travelling on a plane from Fort St. John, BC to Vancouver. He happened to sit next to the only person I had ever met from Fort St. John who also happened to be a business teacher. They talked and he said he was looking for someone to "Canadianize" an American text for use in BC schools. Did she know anyone

who might be interested? She gave him my name. We met and I agreed to do the work. How much did these two jobs provide? Almost exactly the amount we needed. The extra work I'd have to do didn't worry me because the desire was there.

4. Another obstacle which tried to spoil our vacation reared its ugly head just weeks before we were supposed to leave. A month and a half before we were to leave, I came down with mononucleosis. This was the first time in my life I had been seriously ill. Our anniversary was 18 days before we were to leave and I was too sick to celebrate in any way, but I was well enough by July 1 to head out with our friends. I was also too ill to complete the work on the book and I lost 1.5 month's pay from the other position. We had to borrow some of the money, but we paid it back the following year.

5. **<u>We had a wonderful summer!!!!!</u>**

If we could do it, <u>so can you</u>!

NOTES:

Bibliography

You will notice that some of the copyright dates are quite old. However they contain some great material. Many of the authors are still writing today. Check under the author's name and see what you can find.

Briley, Richard Gaylord, *Are You Positive?* New York, Berkeley Books, 1986

Bristol, Claude M., *The Magic of Believing,* Pocket Books, 1977,

Byrne, Rhonda, *The Secret*, Atria Books, 2006

Lebouf, Michael, *Imagineering,* New York, Berkeley Books, 1980

Canfield, Jack, *The Success Principles,* HarperCollins Book Publishers Inc. 2005

Canfield, Jack and Mark Victor Hansen, *The Aladdin Factor,* New York, Berkeley Books, 1995

Canfield, Jack and Mark Victor Hansen, *Dare to Win,* Berkeley Books, 1996

Canfield, Jack and Gay Hendricks, ***You've Got to Read This,*** Harper Collins, 2006

Canfield, Jack and D.D. Watkins, ***Key to Living the Law of Attraction,*** Health Communications, Inc. 2006

Carnegie, Dale**, *How to Win Friends and Influence People,*** Pocket Books, 1967

Carnegie, Dale**, *How to Stop Worrying and Start Living,*** Pocket Books. 1967

Clason, George S.**,*The Richest Man in Babylon,*** Bantam Books, 1985

Conklin, Robert**, *How to Get People to Do Things,*** Ballantine Books, 1984

Conwell, Russell H., ***Acres of Diamonds,*** Spire Books, 1972

Hill, Napoleon and Harold E. Keon, ***Succeed and Grow Rich Through Persuasion,*** Fawcett Crest, *1970*

Hill, Napoleon and W. Clement Stone, ***Success Through a Positive Mental Attitude, Pocket*** Books, 1977

Hill, Napoleon, ***Grow Rich With Peach of Mind,*** Fawcett Crest, 1968

LeBoeuf, Michael, ***Working Smart,*** Warner Books, 1980

Maltz, Maxwell, ***Psycho-Cybernetics and Self-Fulfilling,*** Bantam Books, 1980

Mandino, Og, ***The Choice,*** Bantam Books, 1984

Mandino, Og, ***The Greatest Salesman in the World, Bantam Books, 1985***

Peale, Norman Vincent, ***The Tough Minded Optimist,*** Fawcett Crest, 1967

Peale, Norman Vincent, ***Enthusiasm Makes the Difference,*** Fawcett Books, 1969

Peale, Norman Vincent, ***The Positive Principle Today,*** Fawcett Books, 1976

Schuller, Robert H., ***Discover Your Possibilities,*** Ballantine Books, 1980

Schuller, Robert H., ***You Can Become the Person You Want to Be,*** Hawthorne Books, Inc., 1973

Schwartz, David J. , ***The Magic of Thinking Big,*** Wilshire Book Company, 1971

Sharma Robin, ***The Monk Who Sold His Ferrari,*** Harper Collins, 1964

Stone, W. Clement, ***The Success System That Never Fails,*** Pocket Books, 1980

Waitley, Denis**, *Seeds of Greatness,*** Pocket Books, 1984 Bantam Books, 1985

Waitley, Denis, ***The Joy of Working,*** Ballantine Books, 1986

Waitley, Denis, ***The Psychology of Winning, Berkeley*** Books, 1984

Ziglar, Zig**, *See You at the Top,*** Pelican Publishing, 1977

WHO IS STAN DUNSTER?

Deanna and I have been married for more than 50 years. Even before we got married we decided our two main goals would be to have children and to travel. We now have four children and five grandchildren and have travelled to every province in Canada, 25 states in the USA, and to more than 20 other countries.

This book is based on the steps we took in planning a trip to Europe to celebrate our 25th wedding anniversary.

During the 36 years of my teaching career, including two years teaching for the Canadian Armed Forces in Baden-Baden, Germany, I taught in six secondary schools. I also taught summer classes at Simon Fraser University and at what is now known as BCIT.

For the BC Ministry of Education I served on two curriculum revision committees and created two correspondence courses plus a teachers' manual.

I attained the rank of captain in the Canadian Army Militia.

Deanna and I spent a number of years as tour hosts for several tour-bus operators, visiting locations in Canada, the USA, Britain, Europe, Japan, and Israel.

Many of the ideas I bring to your attention in this book are based on the 12 steps I have used to help us to accomplish the travelling we have done, but these steps can be used in accomplishing any goal you wish.

Our two main life goals when we got married were to have a family and travel. We've done both and we don't intend to stop travelling yet!

Made in the USA
Charleston, SC
12 October 2015